"What Do I Do When...?"

Estate and Financial Action Plans for Life

By:

Linda M. Sekely, Esq.

ISBN: 1-4033-0867-5 (e-book)
ISBN: 1-4033-0868-3 (Paperback)

This book is printed on acid free paper.

1stBooks - rev. 10/01/02

For my two loves—Thom and Adrik

Table Of Chapters

W hat Do I Do When…

Chapters

Introduction

"What do I do when...?"

Wouldn't life be easier if this question could be answered at every turn, every bump, and every curve of our lives? This book is intended to provide some of those answers. Or shall we say, at least provide quick action plans in the estate or financial circumstances described in each chapter.

Of course, the law varies from state to state. You are encouraged to discuss this book with your legal and financial advisors. None of the information contained herein is intended to serve as a substitute for legal advice.

Chapter 1

"What do I do when I graduate?"

Congratulations! You have worked hard, played hard, and come to the end of your education tunnel. Into the light you cross, the light being the real world. Now that you are on your way in your professional career, here is your action plan.

ACTION PLAN

1. **Sign a Will** - You are not too young to have a will. Every adult individual should have one. It can be simple. It is nonetheless crucial.

2. **The Executor** - In your will, choose an executor whom you trust to administer your estate. Often college graduates will select one of their parents to serve in that capacity. We do suggest naming a successor executor other than your parents, just in case a common tragedy should take both of them from you.

3. **Life Insurance** - Examine your need for life insurance. Term policies are generally the most economical. Start with any professional group to which you belong for group rates.

4. **Beneficiary Choice** - For your life insurance policies, employer sponsored retirement plans, and IRA accounts, be sure to list individuals as your primary and secondary beneficiaries. Do not leave these two positions blank or indicate that your estate is the beneficiary. These two selections are the least advantageous from an income tax standpoint.

5. **Insure Your Digs** - Obtain renter insurance on your dwelling and its contents. Be sure that the coverage is adequate to replace the full value of your contents and valuables. Review the insurance contract as you would any important legal document and understand the exclusions.

6. **Be Generous to Yourself** -Maximize your contributions to your employer sponsored retirement plan. Learn to live with less income in favor of this action.

7. **Full Tort** - Be certain to select "full tort" coverage for your automobile. You may wish to consider a higher deductible;

however, you should not consider any coverage less than full tort.

8. **Credit—Watch Your Step** - If you should become overextended in your payment of consumer debt (particularly), do not fail to make a payment in any one-month. If necessary, contact the creditors so they can note in their file that you are making an effort to enter into a payment schedule. Note that you can call and request different due dates for credit cards so that it more closely coincides with your paycheck. If you're swimming under water in this regard, do your homework in the county in which you reside. Often there are consumer credit counseling services located in the counties that will assist in reducing your monthly payments and consolidating your payments into one monthly obligation. Make every effort not to blemish your credit rating by ignoring obligations.

9. **Turn a Decline into a Review** - If you are declined for a credit card, review your credit report. Often there are irregularities and mistakes in the credit report that can be corrected by simple correspondence back to the credit rating agency. Keep a close eye on this report, as it will determine your financial qualification in the future.

10. **<u>Less is More</u>** - Minimize the multiplicity of your major credit cards. Aim at minimizing the total number of credit cards that you have outstanding rather than accepting every offer of credit or applying to several different bank sources.

11. **<u>Just Say No</u>** - No matter how nicely someone asks you, do not co-sign for a loan. Many a tear has been shed from a co-signer who became financially responsible for a debt never believing that that occurrence would arise.

12. **<u>You Are Number One</u>** - Regardless of your size of paycheck, pay yourself first. This refers to setting aside an amount per month that will become your forced savings. This habit can expand as you move into higher income brackets and the savings that you set aside can then become capital ready for investment.

Good habits should start early. View yourself as a business in and of yourself. Paying yourself should be the most important lesson that you hold dear. Saving particularly in qualified retirement plans and IRA's, is not only wise but necessary considering the tenuous future status of social security. The compounding affect of dollars saved early in a career is often referred to as the eighth wonder of the world. We will leave you with this thought: financial and estate planning can be a part of your life no matter what income level you find yourself.

You will never be able to recapture the time that is nigh for planning, for saving. It's your future.

Linda M. Sekely, Esq.

Chapter 2

"What do I do when I get married?"

Walk down the aisle and walk into a solid financial plan for no other reason than peace of mind. Here's your action plan:

ACTION PLAN

1. **Document Check** - Update/prepare your wills. Execute powers of attorney for each other. Make sure they are durable (become irrevocable in the case of incompetency), include medical authorization, and allow for unlimited gifting by your named agent on your behalf.

2. **Trust in a Trust** - Consider executing a life insurance trust which becomes the owner and beneficiary of the life insurance policy owned by you. Why? Because for married couples at the first death there is no tax problem if the wife is the beneficiary. At the wife's death, however, the remaining proceeds are attacked with tax, both state and federal, and probate fees. Why donate that tax money to the government when with 8 pages and the strike of a pen, life insurance proceeds can be removed from all death taxes at <u>both</u> deaths placing more cash in the laps of the children? Sprinkle in the

6

side benefit that the money, while in the trust, can be protected from creditors of the beneficiaries. Yes, your surviving wife/husband may serve as the trustee (with careful drafting) and lifetime beneficiary of that money.

3. **Bypass Magic** - Have your attorney discuss the bypass trust concept with you. Congress grants to all individuals a total of $1,000,000, which can be gifted and willed federal estate tax free. If you and your spouse hold all assets in joint name, at the first death there is no problem. No tax occurs because your spouse may inherit an unlimited amount from you. But, the "bunching effect" happens at the second death. All that cash is heavily taxed. With a few paragraphs in the will, a bypass trust is created that receives up to $1,000,000 of assets in your separate name. The surviving spouse can be the trustee and beneficiary with careful drafting. All income and principal if needed, is paid to the survivor. Here's the kick. All monies in that trust (including earnings) pass tax free to the children at the death of the surviving spouse. Magic! With the use of this tool, up to $2,000,000 can be passed estate tax free to the children. Note that tax legislation is periodically enacted that affects the amount of the $1,000,000.

4. **The Ball—Be Not Dropped** - Don't drop the ball if you include in your Will the bypass trust. Be sure to re-title your assets in the separate names of husband and wife (not joint).

5. **Worksheet** - With attorneys, time is money…your money. So save time and have the following worksheet completed and with you when you arrive at the attorney's office for estate work.

Legal Name (Husband):_____

Legal Name (Wife): _Lois M. Jablon_____

Names/Ages of Children: _Carl Linhart, Jr (1-6-49)_
(5-22-50) Laura Linhart Vantluka
(9-3-53) Janet Linhart
(7-17-54) Gail Anderson

Children from previous marriages:_____

_____

Address: _120 Lynwood Dr_____
Evans City, PA 16033

Phone Number: _____(work)
_724-538-8447_____(home)

County where your reside:_____Butler_____

Executor choice: _LAURALINHART V._ (usually spouse)

Success executor: _CARL LINHART, JR_

Guardian: _____

Successor guardian: _____

Trustee: _____

Successor Trustee: _____

Assets and how titled: _FINANCIAL_ _____

_____

_____

_____

Life Insurance: Face Amount: _____

Owner: _____

Beneficiary: _____

Accounts: Value: _____

Beneficiary: _____

Copy of current will if any (take)

Linda M. Sekely, Esq.

Personal property to go to someone special:_____

___

_____

_____

Ages of children for receiving money in trust—all at age 18 or graduated (e.g. 1/3 at 25, 1/3 at 30, rest at 35)

To whom shall estate go if all your family is deceased? (e.g. ½ to each spouse's families).

_____

_____

Charity?_____

_____

Ask attorney about:

Special Needs Trust if child is disabled

Bypass Trust if your estate is over $1,000,000

Life Insurance Trust if you have a policy over $100,000

Generation Skipping Trust if your estate is over $3,000,000

6. **Inventory—What I have** - Prepare a personal inventory sheet to be kept with your Wills. This is a list of your assts, account

numbers, advisors, policies, etc. Review this yearly on April 15 to be sure of its accuracy. Use the organizer in Chapter 8.

7. **Financial Plan** - Develop your relationship with a Financial Planner. Turn to him/her for cash management, budget development, education savings, risk management, accumulation goals, and estate planning. Balancing all of these interests in today's world is not easy. A financial plan is a systematic integrated plan for dealing with each of these issues.

8. **Life Insurance** - Be sure that you have enough life insurance. Young couples are insuring education of the children and standards of living in the event of premature death. In most instances, term insurance does the trick for the least cost. Following is a chart of insurance types:

Types of Life Insurance Policies

Decreasing Term - Level premium, decreasing coverage, no cash value: Suitable for financial obligations which reduce with time; e.g., mortgages or other amortized loans.

Annual Renewable Term - Increasing premium, level coverage, no cash value: Suitable for financial obligations which remain constant for a short or intermediate period; e.g., income during a minor's dependency.

Long-Term Level Premium Term - Level premium, level coverage, no cash value: The annual premiums are fixed for a period of time, typically 5, 10, 15, or 20 years. Suitable for financial obligations which remain constant for a short or intermediate period; e.g., income during a minor's dependency.

Whole Life - Level premium, level coverage, cash values: Cash value typically increases based on insurance company's general asset account portfolio performance. Suitable for long-term obligations; e.g., surviving spouse lifetime income needs, estate liquidity, death taxes, funding retirement needs, etc.

Universal Life - Level or adjustable premium and coverage, cash values: Cash values may increase, based on the performance of certain assets held in the company's general account. Suitable for long-term obligations or sinking-fund needs: estate growth, estate liquidity, death taxes, funding retirement needs, etc.

<u>Variable Life and Variable Universal Life</u> - Level/adjustable premium, level coverage, cash value: Suitable for long-term obligations and those who are more active investors and for estate growth and death tax liquidity.

<u>Single Premium Whole Life</u> - Entire premium is paid at purchase, cash values, level coverage: Provides protection as well as serving as an asset accumulation vehicle.

9. **<u>Shop, Shop</u>** - Buy a home. Shop for the mortgage. Following is a summary that may help. Explore with your financial planner the wisdom of making your mortgage payment every 2 weeks rather than one full payment every month. A 30-year mortgage may be paid-off in 20 years. In the alternate, make one extra mortgage payment per year and designate it all toward principal with nearly the same affect.

Type	Description
Fixed rate mortgage	Fixed interest rate, usually long-term; equal monthly payments of principal and interest until debt is paid in full.
Fifteen-year mortgage	Fixed interest rate. Requires down payment or monthly payments higher than 30-year loan. Loan is fully repaid in 15 years.

Type	Description
Adjustable rate mortgage	Interest rate changes over the life of the loan, resulting in possible changes in your monthly payments, loan term and/or principal. Some plans have rate of interest caps.
Balloon mortgage	Monthly payments based on fixed interest rate; usually short-term; payments may cover interest only with principal due in full at term end.
Graduated payment mortgage	Lower monthly payments rise gradually (usually over 5-10 years), then level off for duration of term. With adjustable interest rate, additional payment changes possible if index changes.
Assumable mortgage	Buyer takes over seller's original, below-market rate mortgage.
Wraparound	Seller keeps original low rate mortgage. Buyer makes payments to seller who forwards a portion to the lender holding original mortgage. Offers lower effective interest rate on total transaction.
Growing equity mortgage (rapid payoff mortgage)	Fixed interest rate but monthly payments may vary according to agreed-upon schedule or index.
Land contract	Seller retains original mortgage. No transfer of title until loan is fully paid. Equal monthly payments based on below-market interest rate with unpaid principal due at loan end.
Rent with option	Renter pays "option fee" for right to purchase property at specified time and agreed upon price. Rent may or may not be applied to sales price.

10. **Cars, Cars** - Note that in most cases buying the car and not leasing is the more economical way to go. Study the options before signing on the dotted line.

11. **Rentals** - If you have rental property owned by you and your spouse, or separately and have children, consider a family limited partnership. The parents set-up a family limited partnership and deed the property into the partnership. The parents act as general partners. The parents then get to make all decisions regarding the partnership during their lives. The parents gift to the children limited partnership interests. At the end of the day, our goal is that the parents own a small percentage of the total partnership (i.e., 5%) and the vast majority is owned by the children. At the death of the parents, therefore, only 5% of the property value is taxed as an asset of their estate. Two other important advantages of this strategy are noteworthy. First, income generated from the rental is allocated to the partners according to ownership. Income would be allocated out to the children to perhaps be taxed at their lower tax rates. Second, the assets in the partnership are protected from creditors. Watch out for transfer tax in your county and state. Generally, when the property is deeded to the partnership, transfer tax will be due to the county and state (average of 2% of fair market value). In most families, this is

a small price to pay for the dramatic advantages of the partnership.

Your financial and estate plan must breathe with you. Anytime, therefore, you have a change of life circumstance, it merits a look-see at your plan. Here are a few of those circumstances:

> Marriage
> Death of Family Member
> Non-insurability
> Substantial increase in pay
> Birth of child
> New business opened
> Change of heart (heirs)
> Retirement

> Divorce
> Disability
> Move to new state
> Inheritance received
> New job
> Tax law changes
> Death of executor, trustee, guardian
> Divorce

One of the most costly errors is failure to keep Wills, estate plans, and financial plans current. A good rule of thumb is to dust off the estate documents every 2 years at the minimum, review your personal inventory every April 15, and react to a change in life circumstance wisely.

Chapter 3

"What do I do when I have children?"

Congratulations! The little one has arrived by birth or adoption and its time for action.

ACTION PLAN

1. **Wills—Do Them** - Update/prepare your wills including that all-critical guardianship selection for the child. Who is best able to cope with the raising of your minor child? A brother, sister, or friend may be a better choice than grandparents. Factors to consider include: ages of guardian, size of their family, religious affiliation, geographic location, health and wealth. Be sure to name successor guardians also who step up to the plate if the first named guardians are unable or unwilling to serve. Give thought to the turn of events that may occur if the guardians are a couple and may divorce. Hire an experienced attorney to draft your wills, period. This is not the time to turn to "do it yourself" kits and free forms on the Internet. There is too much at stake here. Do not procrastinate. The horror here is if both parents die in a

common disaster, the children (without a will and named guardians) become wards of the state. Interested parties must then at their own legal expense and time petition the court for guardianship. In more circumstances than most, the judge may award guardianship to individuals who would not have been choice #1 of the parents. Further add to the horror—that the children might be placed in foster homes pending the judge's ruling. All of this can be avoided with a few typed pages and a signature. End of lecture.

2. **Trustee Selection** - Most states do not permit minor children to inherit assets outright; therefore, your Will should include a trust to administer their assets. Select a trustee for this purpose. The trustee manages those assets, pays taxes, and makes distributions to the children or their guardians. You will want to name a successor trustee to take the reins in case of the death, resignation, or incapacity of the first trustee.

3. **Beneficiary Status Check** - Check all of your beneficiary designations on life insurance, 401(k) plans, 403(b) plans, IRA's, profit sharing plans and annuities. Primary beneficiary should generally be your spouse. Secondary beneficiary should never be blank or designated as your estate. Your child can be the beneficiary, but the wording should reference the trust in your will for the benefit of a minor child.

4. **Teach Your Children Well** - Start early with savings instruction for the kids. Reward money-smart actions.

5. **Work, Work, Work** - At the age of 14 (the minimum relative to child labor laws in many states), be sure your child is employed in any little job. Do not have him/her paid "under the table". Instruct your child on spending some, saving some, helping others with some. Then open a Roth IRA in his/her name and deposit each year (based on his/her earnings). That cash will grow tax-free, come out tax free to the child eventually, and serve as a last resort emergency fund for education needs. You need not use the child's money to fund the IRA—you may gift the money in.

Chapter 4

"What do I do when I am preparing for my children's education?"

Five words—start as early as possible. There is no need to illustrate here the wonder of the time value of money and the beauty of compounding. Just know that no matter what strategy you embrace, the sooner you start the better.

Funding a college education is generally the largest purchase your family will make, aside from buying your home. The problem is that increasing college costs have, and are expected to, out pace inflation. Lets get to the Action Plan.

ACTION PLAN

1. **Estimate** - You must estimate the amount of annual savings required to pay for college. To do this accurately, see a financial advisor. He is armed with the stats, computer programs, and experience you need to establish this all-important goal line number.

2. **Investing** - Once you recover with the aide of smelling salts upon hearing the estimated nut you must crack, take a breath and determine how your dollars should be invested using automatic monthly deposits if at all possible.

3. **Custodial Accounts** - You may establish an UTMA or UGMA account where the parent is the custodian over an investment/savings account for the benefit of the minor. The problem with this type of account is that the child can reach that money without limitation upon reaching the age of either 18 or 21 depending on your home state.

4. **529 Plan** - There has appeared on the horizon a dramatic and miraculous planning tool in the 529 Plan (named for the section of the Internal Revenue Code that prescribes its features). Very simply, this plan allows donors to contribute to a specific fund for the benefit of Junior with the parent of Junior named as the custodian. Here comes the magic—funds grow tax deferred and are tax-free when taken out for education expenses. That's right, tax-FREE. Be careful in your selection of a 529 Plan—some are restricted with regard to what colleges are permissible. Do your homework, find a solid plan and authorize automatic wiring of a monthly amount from your checking account into the 529 Plan. Select age appropriate growth investments.

5. **IRA** - Try an education IRA on for size. But, note that the above 529 Plans allow for significantly more investing than the IRA.

6. **Savings Bonds** - Series EE savings bonds issued after 1989 may (certain limits apply) be excluded from income if qualified education expenses are paid with redeemed funds. The strategy here is in the rate of return. Historically, savings bonds do not return the most advantageous rate of growth over the long-term.

7. **Strategy** - In general, your investment strategy should be savings placement initially in higher risk investments. As the time for college draws closer, the accumulated bucks should be shifted to more conservative fare. Remember to always match your investments with the time frame you have to invest. The longer the time horizon, the more sense growth oriented investments make.

8. **Trust** - How about a trust? This is the only vehicle that can set aside the cash, remove it from the parents' estates and set forth tailor-made provisions relative to pay-out and age specific guidelines. Throw in the bonus that assets in the trust can be protected from creditor claim, divorce proceedings and

bankruptcy of beneficiaries. Trusts are the way to go if you are aware that your child is not as mature as you wish in the spending of money department. Assets in the trust should be invested in growth stocks—vehicles that postpone income since trust income tax rates are steep. The trustee administers the trust and disperses educational expense money with distribution also permitted for health reasons or maintenance. If you decide to serve as trustee, very careful trust drafting must follow.

9. **<u>Other Doors</u>** - Other resources must include scholarship, financial aid, and part-time employment of the eventual college student. Research the hundreds of scholarship opportunities via the Internet.

10. **<u>When to Do What</u>** - Here is a handy timetable for the kiddos:

   A. Spring of junior year/summer before senior year of high school, narrow college choices and visit campuses.
   B. Investigate scholarships at your colleges and through the high school.
   C. Seek out the application forms for the colleges and due dates.
   D. November - application period begins.

E. December - mail the CSS profile and keep gathering financial aid information.

F. January - apply for financial aid every year at this time, complete and mail FASFA (Free Application for Federal Student aid) and apply for scholarships.

G. February - student aid report will be received. Review it and make changes. Submit documents to financial aid offices.

H. March - Receive financial aid award letters.

I. May - make college decision and send deposits.

J. August - start college and get on-campus job.

This is a time for action - investment action by parents at the birth or adoption of your child, and attention to detail by the child as college draws closer. The importance of your financial planner's advice cannot be overemphasized. There is no time to waste in this game of education and, as we all know, 18 years pass in two blinks of an eye.

Chapter 5

"What do I do when I am caring for a widowed parent?"

The wheels of time turn, like it or not. One day you wake up and the rules have changed. You are caring for an aging parent. Here's the list:

ACTION PLAN

1. **Time to Update** - Trouble can be found when the widowed parent states that she has a will that she signed 20 years ago with her husband. You must guide her to execute an updated will. You may be named as executor and want to pave the way for this job with solid estate documents.

2. **Power of Attorney** - Especially crucial for the aging parent is to execute a power of attorney now, while there is no competency or medical emergency issues. Be sure that it specifically allows for the sale and conveyance of real estate and gifting authorization. Be sure that it is durable (becomes irrevocable upon incompetency) and allows for unlimited

gifting. Even if all financial accounts are jointly owned with you and Mom, a power of attorney is still needed for medical authority. Have it drafted by an attorney. There is too much to lose if it is defective.

3. **Review Titling of Assets** - Many widowed parents place title to assets in joint name with one or more children. This generally can save inheritance tax (taxed on only the parent's portion), but watch out for state law. Some states require full tax in Mom's estate if the money was originally all hers. Second caveat—if assets are in joint name, generally the co-owner child can access the funds and creditors of that person can reach the accounts. Caution, if one of the children on the joint account should predecease Mom, Mom could pay death tax on her own money. The good news is jointly titled assets generally escape probate fees and pass automatically to the joint holder upon the death of Mom. Mom should understand that no matter what she indicates in her will, that asset goes to the joint holder at her death.

4. **The Abode** - The house is an often-asked query. Should Mom convey the house to the children? Two-word answer—it depends. The often forgotten mathematical comparison that must be done centers around the eventual sale of the house after the parent's death. If the house is deeded to the children

during the parent's life, the children take as their own the low cost basis paid for the house (plus improvements) by the parent. If the children eventually sell the house, they will pay capital gains tax on the difference between the sale price and that low cost. Capital gain rate is generally 20%. You must compare that estimated capital gain amount to the inheritance tax rate applied to the house if it remains in the name of the parent until his/her death. In Pennsylvania for example, the inheritance tax rate is only 4.5%, a far less rate than the capital gain rate. Then, when the children eventually sell the house, they will likely pay no capital gain because they have inherited the house at a basis of the fair market value on the date of death. The sale price is usually equal to that figure or very close to it. So you see, the answer "it depends" is accurate.

5. **P.O.D.** - When the parent wishes to keep full control over his/her assets up to the moment of death, the parent could elect to title assets "POD", payable on death. No tax is saved, but those assets generally do not pass through probate.

6. **Gifting** - The parent should be encouraged to gift—to remove assets from his/her estate (along with the appreciation on those assets). You know the drill. Up to $11,000 per person per year can be gifted by the parent without gift or estate tax

effect. Consider using trusts as receptacles if outright gifting is not favored. The parent can then design the term of the trust and, in effect, exercise control from beyond the grave. Gifts made prior to death avoid probate but may be brought back into the parent's estate for death tax purposes. Consult your state's laws on this. In Pennsylvania for example, you must live for one year from the date of the gift. For federal estate tax purposes, you must live 3 years.

7. **Living Trust** - See the section in Chapter 7 regarding this tool.

8. **Prepay Burial Expenses** - Many parents wish to prepay burial expenses either to the funeral home or via a burial trust at a bank. The advantage of prepaying to the funeral home is that prices are frozen on that date.

9. **Update, Again** - Update beneficiary selection on the surviving parent's retirement accounts, life insurance, annuities, etc. This is often overlooked and of course, after death, it is too late.

10. **Charity** - Discuss charitable inclinations with the parent and make sure that the bequest makes it to the Will itself to insure tax deductibility.

11. **<u>Living Will</u>** - Have the surviving parent execute a living will which serves as a directive to the physician in the case of life support measures. Not only does this document help to ease the burden of her family, but also smoothes the issues surrounding at-home hospice care.

There is a growing faction of attorneys that concentrate in elder law. No doubt this is in reaction to our aging population and prolonged life span. The good news is there is plenty of quality assistance out there waiting to address special issues that may arise related to such subjects as asset protection, social security, disability, guardianship, or competency.

Chapter 6

"What do I do when I am named as Executor or Executrix?"

A good friend or a member of your family is having a will drawn up, and asks you whether you would be willing to act as the executor. You feel honored by this request, and give your consent. Or, perhaps someone close to you has passed away and the time has come to assume your executorial function. You may be wondering exactly what the extent of your obligations will be, how much time your duties may demand, and where to go for help in fulfilling this important role.

This chapter is intended to give you an overview of the estate administration process in general, focusing on the executor's responsibilities to gather estate information, pay debts, expenses, and taxes, and distribute the assets of the estate in accordance with the wishes of the deceased. It is, of course, not intended as a substitute for legal or tax advice. It will, however, give you an idea of the duties that you will be performing as you go through probate and help you to be an informed client if you hire professionals to perform some of these tasks.

First, don't be intimidated by the phrase "Go Through Probate". Probate merely refers to the series of legal procedures by which a state government attempts to see that the debts, taxes, and expenses of its deceased residents will be paid with the remaining assets accurately distributed to the rightful heirs or beneficiaries. A court in the county in which the decedent lived oversees these described procedures. Note that it is generally immaterial where the decedent owns property or was physically located at death. Instead, the county in which the decedent lived marks the location of the probate process.

As the executor, you have the right to hire experts to help you undergo probate and complete your other duties. You are also entitled to charge their reasonable fees to the estate. The size and the complexity of the estate, as well as your own level of expertise in handling financial and tax matters, will determine the extent to which you will need the assistance of an attorney, accountant, investment advisor or tax practitioner.

Often the executor will silently wonder whether he or she is entitled to receive compensation for the performance of their duties. Besides reimbursement for all of your out-of-pocket expenses, you will be entitled to receive a fee for your own services as executor. In most states the executor's commission is stated as a percentage of the estate's assets, and is set by law or case law. In the alternative, many states merely provide for reasonable fees with the reasonableness to be determined by the court. You can, however, choose to waive part or all of this fee if you so desire. Note that if you do collect a fee for the execution of your duties, that fee is taxable on your individual income tax return as miscellaneous income.

Linda M. Sekely, Esq.

Now that the preliminary information has been set forth, let's move on to our action list.

ACTION LIST

1. **<u>Don't Be Afraid to Ask</u>** - If an individual has named you as executor and is still alive, tactfully gather as much information as possible so that your duty later is made easier. At the very least, ask the person (referred to as the testator) who has named you in his will for the location of the will and his other important documents.

2. **<u>Know the Will's Location</u>** - Given the best of circumstances, the testator may give you a copy of the will in a sealed envelope to be opened upon his death. He may instead give you merely a copy of the will. If this is the case, make sure that you know exactly where to find the original will. Only the original will can be probated after death.

3. **<u>Where to Look</u>** - If you are named as an executor check the following places for the original will:

   - First, check the safe deposit box or boxes under the name of the deceased. Bank officials will allow you to enter into the safe deposit box in their presence if you have a certified death certificate and are examining the box merely for the reason of ascertaining whether a will is located in the box.

- Second, check the residence for a firebox or safe.
- Third, ask relatives and the deceased's lawyer.
- Fourth, move on to the personal files of the deceased.

4. **Burial Wishes** - The executor is often charged with carrying out the burial wishes of the deceased. You can imagine that the will is the worst place to indicate burial wishes. From a practical standpoint, many wills are not reviewed until well after the body has been interred. As mentioned above, the bank official will not allow you to enter into a safe deposit box until a death certificate is reviewable by the bank official. Death certificates require some number of days for ordering by the funeral home director. Therefore, if you know that you are named as an executor, be sure to ask the testator if he has any particular burial wishes that can be communicated to you during life.

5. **A Road Map to the Assets** - Determine if the testator prepared a letter of instruction or some other road map as to where assets can be found. If no such letter is found, gather the latest mail of the deceased to investigate account statements, bank statements, credit card bills, etc. This

investigation will at least give you some idea as to current debts and assets.

6. **Mail** - Have the mail forwarded to your name and address from the deceased's mailing address.

7. **Social Security** - Notify social security of the death of the deceased. If this step is overlooked, the estate will be required to refund excess social security payments made to the deceased.

8. **The Funeral** - Assist in the funeral arrangements if necessary. The surviving spouse or family members rather than the executor generally make these arrangements. The deceased's wishes should be respected if they are known.

9. **Save All Receipts** - The executor is not personally responsible for paying the funeral bills and other expenses, however, the executor is responsible for keeping track of expenses and providing the tax preparer with the information that will be deductible to the estate. If you do not have a computerized or systemized method in which to keep track of expenses, save receipts in a box or file. Additionally, if you pay any expenses on behalf of the estate out of your checkbook for convenience purposes, make a note of those expenses, and save the

cancelled check, invoice or receipt that indicates the nature of the expense.

10. **Expenses** - Virtually all expenses paid for the purposes of burial or cremation of the body are deductible. This includes the wake, fees to the clergy, organist fees, cost of flowers, all funeral costs, cost of the cemetery marker, perpetual care, and the costs of travel, meals and lodging for the person who is in charge of making the funeral arrangements. Funeral expenses are given priority when an estate has limited assets. Under the laws of most states, funeral expenses are paid before any other obligations, except expenses of administration such as court costs, attorney fees, and executor fees.

11. **Death Certificates** - Order several copies (minimum of 10) of the certified death certificates through the funeral director. That is the easiest way in which to obtain copies. Death certificates must be original in order to be used, with copying of the same not permitted. If additional death certificates are needed during the administration of the estate, additional death certificates can be obtained from the County Health Department or the Bureau of Vital Records in your state. It often is the case, however, that the funeral director can order additional death certificates in a more timely fashion. As to the number of death certificates required, you will generally

need a separate certified death certificate in order to transfer each piece of real estate, motor vehicle, stock certificate, bank account, etc. You also need a death certificate for the probating of the estate and for each life insurance policy that requires processing.

12. **Locate and Read the Will** - As you read it, obtain from family members the names, addresses and phone numbers of all individuals named in the will. Hollywood has portrayed the "reading of the will" as a dramatic sequence after the individual's death. This is not required. The probate process does however require notice to all individuals named in the will. The attorney administering the estate will perform this task. It is, however, your job to supply the attorney with the names, addresses and phone numbers of the beneficiaries.

13. **Hiring the Attorney** - Retain the services of an attorney for the administration of the estate. Do not be shy in negotiating your fee with the attorney. Suggest that the attorney charge you the lesser of his hourly fee or the prescribed reasonable fee for your estate. Volunteer to do much of the work yourself. Always keep communications with the attorney concise and the information that you provide to him accurate and clear. Further, ask that the attorney to give you a time line as to the probate process.

14. **<u>Swearing In</u>** - The attorney will accompany you to the
probate court in the appropriate county. There, the attorney
will present a brief petition to the court and a clerk will swear
you in as the executor of the estate. This is generally not done
in a courtroom but before a clerk's desk. The clerk will issue
you the court appointed certificate that names you as the
executor of the estate. You and your attorney will want to
order several of these certificates at that time. Generally one
of these certificates is needed in each of the circumstances
listed above regarding death certificates. This certificate
contains the seal of the court; therefore, copies of the
certificate are not used. Generally certificates can be issued as
you wait.

15. **<u>Publishing</u>** - The attorney will handle the publishing of the
estate in the local newspapers as required by your state law.
Your name will be included in the publishing as the
representative of the estate. This is for the purposes of
creditor notification.

16. **<u>Estate Account</u>** - You will establish an estate checking
account. You will need to have a tax identification number
from the IRS. The account should be opened under a name
such as "Estate of Mary Doe, John Doe, Executor." You will

be the authorized signator on the account. The court appointed document will be necessary to present to the bank.

17. **<u>Your Powers</u>** - You now have the legal authority and the responsibility to conduct the decedent's business affairs as he or she would have done, had death not occurred. However, there are a few restrictions on your powers. You have the duty to use care and skill that an ordinarily prudent person would use with respect to his or her own affairs. This is referred to as fiduciary duty. You will want to use this standard in your duties of marshalling assets and liquidating and distributing them as easily as possible.

18. **<u>How Long?</u>** - The total period of an administration from time of death to final closing typically ranges from six to eighteen months.

19. **<u>Updates</u>** - You will want to request from the attorney periodic status letters that you can share with the beneficiaries. Note that under all state laws the beneficiaries have the right to examine the records and books of the estate as it is being administered. You should therefore, remain polite and professional with regard to any requests made by beneficiaries.

20. **Taxes, Taxes** - You will be responsible for filing and paying applicable federal and state taxes which include income taxes of the decedent, estate taxes, and inheritance taxes for the particular state. These taxes must be filed on a timely basis. Note however, that extensions are available for all of these returns. You will want to mark accordingly on your calendar the due dates so that you can monitor the meeting of the deadlines. The federal and most state tax returns are due nine months from the date of death. Note that extensions are possible and most states provide for a discount if the return is filed or a prepayment is made early.

21. **Notice to the IRS** - Upon assuming the role of executor, a decedent's representative should notify the IRS of his capacity in acting for the estate on Form 56, Notice Concerning Fiduciary Relationship. Filing this form is not mandatory, but it is suggested if you live at an address that is different from that of the deceased. Until this form is received, the IRS will continue to send the decedent's mail, including any important tax notices or notices of audit to his or her former address.

22. **To Serve and Protect** - You will need to protect estate assets, by way of insurance or by taking valuable papers, cash, securities and jewelry into your custody. You must provide for

the protection and security of vacant real estate. The locks to the real estate should be changed.

23. **List the Assets** - You must determine the full nature and value of the assets of the deceased and compile a list including the value of all real estate, and a summary of outstanding mortgages, leases and other encumbrances. An appraisal should be arranged for real estate or other valuables if needed. You should collect and examine existing insurance policies on real estate household contents, automobiles, etc. and determine that the insurance is accurate. An excellent source of information is the decedent's checkbook and file of cancelled checks. Look for payments made for investments, insurance, debts, mortgages, medical expenses, tax payments, and safe deposit box rental fees.

24. **Assets—What are Counted?** - Under federal tax law, all of the property owned by the decedent anywhere in the world, even property of which he owned only a fractional share, must be counted. The value must be determined as of the date of death. Note that an alternative date of six months after the date of death may be elected for federal estate tax purposes. In order to qualify for this alternative valuation date, the subject assets cannot be liquidated. or transferred to heirs. The value of all property is its fair market value. IRS

regulations define fair market value as "the price at which the property would change hands between a willing buyer and a willing seller."

25. **For Business, the Beat Must Go On** - If a business is involved, arrange for the continuity and proper management. The valuation of a closely held business interest should be arranged.

26. **Employee Benefits—Find Them and Claim Them** - Contact the place of work of the deceased to inquire with regard to pensions and life insurance coverage.

27. **Debts—Who Gets Paid and What?** - Determine what debts the deceased owed at the time of death and arrange for payment of them. Again, you may advance for the estate payment of the debts to be reimbursed at a later date. You should contact the creditors immediately. Often, payment plans can be negotiated pending the final closing of the estate. If the estate is insolvent, you should consult with the attorney before paying any of the creditors in full. There is in each state a designated order of creditors for insolvent estates.

28. **Safe Deposit Box** - If the decedent had a safe deposit box, many states require the State Department of Revenue to be

present at an inventory of the box. You should attend this box opening. The contents will be handed to you for safekeeping.

29. **Start the Flurry of Claim Forms** - File claims for Medicare, private medical insurance, veteran's burial benefits, and life insurance claims. Most life insurance claim forms can be obtained on the web. Obtain the IRA claim forms and distribute them to the beneficiary named.

30. **Time To Deal Out The Assets** - You will distribute the remaining assets. Often, advanced distributions are made to beneficiaries. Be sure to keep close records of such distributions. Of course, the instructions in the will govern the process of distribution. In addition, you must follow whatever procedures are required by the probate court in your situation. The attorney will be required to file a final accounting in most situations. The closing of the estate is on the duty roster of the attorney whether accomplished by a formal petition to the court or informally through a settlement agreement signed by all heirs.

As you can see, the role of the executor is an important one, involving a wide variety of skills and requiring you to make decisions that can affect the lives of survivors for many years to come. Nevertheless the job is manageable, if you follow the steps outlined above and consult with experienced professionals as needed. You should be able to proceed with confidence, knowing that when your tasks are complete and the estate is closed, you will have honored the memory of your friend or loved one in a meaningful way.

Chapter 7

"What do I do when my spouse dies?"

No matter how prepared you may be for the death of your spouse, particularly in light of advances of medical science and appropriate planning, it is comforting to know that there is an appropriate and orderly fashion in which you should proceed. We like to believe that by providing you with the following thoughts and ideas, your grieving period can be made a bit easier.

Following the notification to friends and loved ones of a death, the first impending procedure is that of the funeral arrangements. Coming from a place of research, common sense, and war stories, we have listed below an action plan with regard to the making of funeral arrangements.

ACTION PLAN

1. **Preplanning** - If you have preplanned your funeral arrangements, be sure to follow the location instructions of the preplanning. Check the preplanning contract to be sure that you understand your choices with regard to planning through that chosen funeral home or transferring the options to another home.

2. **Shop Around** - Approach this procedure as an informed consumer. Don't be hesitant to shop around.

3. **Price List** - Before discussing anything with the funeral director, request his price list for services (often referred to as their basic service fees). The basic service fee usually includes the charge for doing business with the funeral home and includes many of the other services provided such as refrigeration, embalming, use of the facility and the memorial service, just to name a few. If the funeral director refuses to give you the basic service fee schedule or information, choose another facility. There is no excuse for not providing this information.

4. **Forethought** - Sit down at home and figure out what you want and can afford without having the funeral director indicate to you what you can and cannot do.

5. **Insurance** - Never mention that you have life insurance. There is no requirement that you show any policy. A trick question used to be "how many copies of the death certificate do you need for life insurance purposes?" This was an indirect way of ascertaining whether you did have life insurance and the price could be increased as a result. Your

response should just be "I need ten copies of the death certificate for the estate administration purposes".

6. **Moving On** - Do not be rushed into a quick decision with regard to the funeral arrangements. If one funeral home picks up the body and you decide to move your spouse to another funeral home due to price or arrangement considerations, the funeral home cannot hold the body for ransom. That is against the law, the same as kidnapping. Even if you signed a contract with the funeral home, you have seventy-two hours to cancel it in most states.

7. **Keep the Crowd Small** - Do not include a large number of family members or the clergy at the making of the arrangements. The more the number of those present, the more the services complicate and the cost will often run up. Remember that this is a sales conference. Keep the attending family members to a minimum.

8. **Counseling Caution** - Be aware of the after service "grief counseling". This may be an opportunity to sell you a pre-need package.

9. **Ask, Ask, Ask** - Be sure that you understand when the funeral home sells you a "complete package". Do not be afraid to ask

several questions so that you understand fully the terms of the contract.

10. **<u>Cremation</u>** - Be aware that a casket is not required for a direct cremation. The only requirement is that it meets the standard set by the crematory. If this is the selection for your spouse, enter into a frank discussion with regard to the costs and requirement for this type of disposition.

11. **<u>Itemize</u>** - Request that the funeral director provide you with an itemized accounting of all goods and services selected and to be provided. Of course, save that itemized accounting as well as all receipts and cancelled checks.

Often, the surviving spouse will be named in the will as the executor or executrix. See Chapter 6 for the suggested procedures for that role.

During the administration of the estate and shortly thereafter, you will want to review the beneficiary designations of the following assets and change the primary and secondary beneficiary designations accordingly. So often this review and change is overlooked by the surviving spouse.

- IRA accounts
- Life insurance policies on your life

- 401K plans or other qualified employer sponsored retirement plans
- Annuities
- Any other assets which require a beneficiary designation

Very careful planning is required with respect to IRA designations for surviving spouses. Not only does the beneficiary designation determine what individual or charity will ultimately receive the benefit of the IRA account, but such beneficiary designation also determines how the minimum distribution will be calculated for payment to the surviving spouse upon her reaching of age 70½. Note that certain designations that you make with regard to IRA accounts are irrevocable once you reach age 70½. Suffice it to say that very careful planning in this area is required.

The surviving spouse is required to begin distributions from the deceased spouse's IRA by December 31st of the year following the spouse's death. Be sure to respect that date and monitor this very important step.

Into the forefront of estate planning has come the term "post mortem planning". This term refers to the estate planning that takes place by the surviving spouse focusing on her own planning needs. The following estate planning tools should be considered by you:

- A New Will

    A new will should be drafted.

48

- Beneficiaries

  The beneficiary designations indicated above should be made. The same care should be taken when selecting the beneficiary designations as the degree of care used in drafting a will.

- Power of Attorney

  A power of attorney should be drafted for you. This power of attorney should be "durable" in nature. This indicates that the power of attorney would be irrevocable if you would become incapacitated. Generally one of your children is selected as your agent. In plain language, the power of attorney allows the agent to step into your shoes when needed. Medical authority should be included.

- Living Will

  A living will should be considered. In most states the living will is a medical directive which addresses the needs and wishes of the declarant with regard to life sustaining procedures. In practical terms, the primary reason why this document is valuable is to lessen the burden on family members with regard to these very critical decisions. A copy of the living will should be filed with the primary care physician of the surviving spouse.

- Review Your Assets

    All of your assets should be reviewed, particularly with regard to how assets are titled. For example, depending on your asset mix and the estate plan of your child or children, real estate may be re-titled in joint name with you and your child. This would reduce the estate and inheritance tax bill in half if carefully designed. Many parents favor this re-titling, because the parent is still on the deed for purposes of control during life. Any re-titling of real estate must be weighed against the loss of the step-up in basis that occurs. This refers to the fact that making a gift of property transfers to the recipient of the gift the basis (the cost which the surviving spouse paid for the property plus improvement) to the recipient. Contrast this to the "step-up" in basis that occurs if the property would have remained in your sole name. The value of the property would be fixed at the fair market value for purposes of the inheritance tax and for the subsequent sale of the property to a third party buyer. The benefit of the step-up in basis is that the heirs generally would owe no capital gains tax on the subsequent sale of the property. In summary on this point, do not proceed with re-titling of real estate prior to full analysis of whether this makes sense in your particular family's situation.

- <u>Gifting</u>

    Consider a gifting program to children and grandchildren. The goal of this program is to remove assets, particularly if the assets are ones that will appreciate in value, from your estate. Every estate should consider a gifting strategy. You can gift up to $11,000 per recipient per year without any gift tax reporting or consequences. If your gifting includes gifts to grandchildren, a common strategy is to place those cash gifts into a trust for the benefit of the grandchild. The benefits of this include protection from creditors of the grandchild, protection from too much control on the part of the grandchild, and your ability to dictate the payment terms from the trust. When considering the gifting strategy, be sure to explore with a professional the many ways that gifts can be given while still retaining some managerial authority over the asset. Carefully drafted trusts are ideal for this purpose.

- <u>Revocable Trust/Living Trust</u>

    Consider revocable trusts. A revocable or sometimes referred to as "living" trust, re-titles your property into the name of a trust which is cancelable at any time by you. Generally you are named as the trustee of the trust with full authority to pay out income or principle as needed to yourself or to your creditors. Why do it then you may ask? The revocable trust provides three benefits in general. First, the utilization of this type of trust saves in probate fees. Probate refers specifically to the fees that are owed to the county of residence of the deceased for the probating of the estate and the cost of administration of the estate including the executor fees and the attorney fees. Assets that are re-titled in the name of the revocable trust are not probate assets. As non-probate assets they are not included in the calculation of the probate fees. Second, the revocable trust allows the estate to be administered more quickly than through the probate process in general. The trust indicates where the property will be distributed after your death. A successor trustee "takes the reins" of the trust and distributes the property as designated by you. Third, the revocable trust is generally not filed with the probating court. It is a private document and therefore the terms of the trust are not reviewable by the public as are the terms of a will which is filed and made of public record. Be careful with these animals. The marketing of the revocable trust in a package of estate planning documents has become the flavor of the year for many estate planners. Caution is required in this area because in many states the cost of probate is not exorbitant or even worthy of the cost of creating the revocable trust. Also note that a popular misconception is that this type of trust saves inheritance or estate tax. It does not! In the right circumstance this estate planning tool is very appropriate. In particular it is very useful if you wish to keep control over your assets, however want to guard against incapacitation. The terms of the trust can indicate that upon incapacity the successor trustee immediately takes over the management of the assets. As with any estate planning tool or strategy, it boils down to what is best for the particular estate.

Losing a spouse is indeed a financial, emotional, and generally overwhelming event. It is impossible to suggest the exact estate planning tools that should be utilized by every surviving spouse. To do so would be folly. Every estate is as unique as the individual. At least, by reviewing the above concerns, the more overlooked procedures are brought to the forefront. We can with confidence leave you with this thought: Don't **panic.** The world abounds with quality professionals who can guide you through this difficult transitional period. Seek them out based mostly on personal recommendation of others, ask many questions concerning their fees, and be forthright with them concerning your desires.

Chapter 8

"What Do I Do When I Need to Get Organized?"

The following pages give you what you need—a detailed Personal Affairs Organizer to keep with your Will and other important documents. A three-ring binder works well as a holder of all the data.

PERSONAL ORGANIZER

Linda M. Sekely, Esq.

PERSONAL DATA

Full Name:_____(Maiden)_____

Address: _____

_____

Phone: H: (   ) _____ W: (   ) _____

Birthdate:_____ Place of Birth:_____

Citizen of:_____

Social Security#:____ / ___ / ___ Medicare #:_____

Spouse:_____(Maiden)_____

Birthdate:_____ Place of Birth:_____

Citizen of:_____

Military Service:_____ Military Service #:_____

Service From:____To:_____ Discharge Date:_____

Rank:_____ Recognition:_____

56

CHILDREN

Name: _____

Address: _____

_____

Telephone:_____

Birthdate:_____ Social Security #:_____/_____/_____

Name: _____

Address: _____

_____

Telephone:_____

Birthdate: _____ Social Security #:_____

Name: _____

Address: _____

_____

Telephone:_____

Birthdate:_____ Social Security #:_____/_____/_____

Addresses are current as of the following date:_____

Linda M. Sekely, Esq.

JOB DATA

Employer:_____

Address:_____

_____

Telephone:_____   Fax: _____

Contact Person:_____   Dept. _____

Position with Company:_____

Date of Hire: _____   Retirement Date:_____

Employee Benefits: (such as retirement plan, death benefits, insurance, accumulated leave, stock options, etc.)

_____

_____

Employer:_____

Address:_____

_____

Telephone:_____   Fax: _____

Contact Person:_____   Dept. _____

Position with Company:_____

Date of Hire: _____   Retirement Date:_____

Employee Benefits: (such as retirement plan, death benefits, insurance, accumulated leave, stock options, etc.)

_____

Linda M. Sekely, Esq.

SPOUSE'S JOB

Employer:_____

Address:_____

Telephone:_____   Fax:_____

Contact Person:_____   Dept. _____

Position with Company: _____

Date of Hire: _____   Retirement Date:_____

Employee Benefits: (such as retirement plan, death benefits,

insurance, accumulated leave, stock options, etc.)

_____

_____

Employer:_____

Address:_____

_____

Telephone:_____   Fax:_____

Contact Person:_____   Dept._____

Position with Company:_____

Date of Hire: _____   Retirement Date:_____

Employee Benefits: (such as retirement plan, death benefits, insurance, accumulated leave, stock options, etc.)

_____

_____

Linda M. Sekely, Esq.

BANK SAFE DEPOSIT BOX

Do you have a Safety Deposit Box? _____ (Y/N)

Located: _____

Address:_____

Box #_____ Date Paid through:_____

Keys are Located:_____

Individuals Authorized to access the box:_____

List of Contents:_____

_____

POST OFFICE BOX

Do you have a Post Office Box? _____ (Y/N)

Located:_____

Address:_____

Box # _____ Date Paid through:_____

Keys are Located/Combination:_____

Individuals Authorized to access the box:_____

CONTACT PAGE

	Name	**Phone**
Accountant	_____	_____
Financial Planner	_____	_____
Attorney	_____	_____
Banker	_____	_____
Religious Leader	_____	_____
Physician	_____	_____
Executor	_____	_____
Co-Executor (if any)	_____	_____
Successor Executor	_____	_____
Trustee	_____	_____
Co-Trustee (if any)	_____	_____
Successor Trustee	_____	_____
Attorney-in-Fact under Durable	_____	_____
Power of Attorney	_____	_____
Attorney-in-Fact under Health	_____	_____
Care Power of Attorney	_____	_____

Linda M. Sekely, Esq.

Attorney-in-Fact under Living   _____   _____

Living Will   _____   _____

Your Legal Guardian   _____   _____

Other   _____   _____

MEDICAL

Medical Doctor:_____ Name of Practice:_____

Address:_____

Telephone:_____

Medical Doctor:_____ Name of Practice:_____

Address:_____

Telephone:_____

LIVING WILL

The Living Will is a document intended to state your intentions regarding life-supporting procedures that will artificially prolong your life, when there exists no plausible chances of recovery.

Do you have a Living Will? _____(Y/N)

Location of Original:_____ Copies:_____

Name of Surrogate:_____ Relation to you:_____

DURABLE POWER OF ATTORNEY

The Durable Power of Attorney allows a designated individual to make decisions on your behalf in the event you become incapacitated or incapable of making your own decisions.

Do you have a Durable Power of Attorney? _____(Y/N)

Location of Original:_____ Copies:_____

Name of Agent:_____ Relation to you:_____

HEALTHCARE POWER OF ATTORNEY

The Health Care Power of Attorney allows a designated individual to make medical and health related decisions that are not life and death decisions on your behalf, in the event that you become incapacitated or incapable of making a decision.

Do you have a health care power of attorney?_____(Y/N)

Location of original:_____   Copies:_____

Name of attorney in Fact:_____Relation to you:_____

ANATOMICAL GIFT

This document allows you to designate particular organs for purposes of transplants, education, the advancement of science, etc.

Do you have an Anatomical Gift Document? _____(Y/N)

Location:

_____

(Please provide copies of the above documents if available)

Linda M. Sekely, Esq.

MEDICAL (SPOUSE)

Medical Doctor:_____ Name of Practice:_____

Address:_____

Telephone:_____

Medical Doctor:_____ Name of Practice:_____

Address:_____

Telephone:_____

LIVING WILL

The Living Will is a document intended to state your intentions regarding life-supporting procedures that will artificially prolong your life, when there exists no plausible chances of recovery.

Do you have a Living Will?   _____(Y/N)

Location of Original:_____ Copies:_____

Name of Surrogate:_____ Relation to you:_____

DURABLE POWER OF ATTORNEY

The Durable Power of Attorney allows a designated individual to make decisions on your behalf in the event that you become incapacitated or incapable of making your own decisions.

Do you have a Durable Power of Attorney? _____(Y/N)

Location of Original:_____ Copies:_____

Name of Agent:_____ Relation to you:_____

HEALTHCARE POWER OF ATTORNEY

The Health Care Power of Attorney allows a designated individual to make medical and health related decisions that are not life and death decisions on your behalf, in the event that you become incapacitated or incapable of making a decision.

Do you have a health care power of attorney?_____(Y/N)

Location of original:_____   Copies:_____

Name of attorney in Fact:_____   Relation to you:_____

ANATOMICAL GIFT

This document allows you to designate particular organs for purposes of transplants, education, the advancement of science, etc.

Do you have an Anatomical Gift Document? _____(Y/N)

Location:
_____
(Please provide copies of the above documents if available)

LAST REQUESTS

_____ My burial requests are as follows:

Cemetery: _____

Location:_____

Telephone: _____

Did you prepurchase a burial plot? _____(Y/N)

Location of plot Certificate of Ownership:_____

Have Burial Costs been pre-paid? _____(Y/N)

Funeral Home: _____

Funeral Director: _____ Telephone:_____

I have Burial Insurance _____(Y/N) Policy #:_____

Insurance Company: _____
(Please attach copy of policy)

Other Information:_____
(perpetual care, Headstone, Inscription, etc.)

_____

_____

_____ I wish to be cremated. Please follow these instructions:

_____

_____

Linda M. Sekely, Esq.

LAST REQUESTS (SPOUSE)

_____ My burial requests are as follows:

Cemetery:_____

Location:_____

Telephone: _____

Did you prepurchase a burial plot?   _____(Y/N)

Location of plot Certificate of Ownership:_____

Have Burial Costs been pre-paid?   _____(Y/N)

Funeral Home: _____

Funeral Director: _____ Telephone:_____

I have Burial Insurance _____(Y/N) Policy #:_____

Insurance Company: _____
(Please attach copy of policy)

Other Information:_____
(perpetual care, Headstone, Inscription, etc.)

_____

_____

_____ I wish to be cremated. Please follow these instructions:

_____

_____

74

TRUSTS

Name of Trust:_____

Date Signed:_____

Grantor:_____ Trustee:_____

Prepared by:_____

Telephone:_____

Original Document is located:_____

Funded with the following assets:_____

_____

_____

(Please enclose a copy of the Trust Document if available)

WILL

Last Date Will was Signed:_____

Last Date Codicil was Signed:_____

Executor:_____

Prepared by:_____

Telephone:_____

Original Document is located:_____

Copies are located:_____

TRUSTS

Name of Trust:_____

Date Signed:_____

Grantor:_____ Trustee:_____

Prepared by:_____

Telephone:_____

Original Document is located:_____

Funded with the following assets:_____

_____

_____

(Please enclose a copy of the Trust Document if available)

WILL (SPOUSE)

Last Date Will was Signed:_____

Last Date Codicil was Signed:_____

Executor:_____

Prepared by:_____

Telephone:_____

Original Document is located:_____

Copies are located:_____

TRUSTS FOR CHILDREN/GRANDCHILDREN

Name of Trust:_____

Date Trust Signed:_____

Prepared by: _____

Telephone: _____

Original Document is located:_____

Grantor(s):_____ Trustee(s):_____

Beneficiaries:_____

(Please enclose a copy of the Trust Document if available)

CHARITABLE TRUSTS

Name of Trust:_____

Date Trust Signed:_____

Prepared by:_____

Telephone:_____

Original Document is located:_____

(Please enclose a copy of the Trust Document if available)

Linda M. Sekely, Esq.

INSURANCE TRUSTS

Date Trust Signed:_____   Date Policy Issued:_____

Grantor(s):_____   Trustee(s):_____

Insurance Company:_____

Telephone:_____

Policy #:_____   Face Amount $_____

Original Document is located:_____

(Please enclose a copy of the Trust Document if available)

OTHER TRUSTS

Creator of Trust:_____

Date Trust Signed:_____

Contact Person:_____

Telephone:_____

My interest in this Trust is:_____

_____

_____

_____

INSURANCE

LIFE INSURANCE POLICIES

Effective Date:_____

Policy #:_____   Amount of Death Benefit:$_____

Insurance Company:_____

Address:_____

Telephone:_____

Insurance Agent:_____

Telephone:_____

Location of Policy:_____

(Please enclose a copy of the Insurance policy if available)

Effective Date:_____

Policy #:_____   Amount of Death Benefit:$_____

Insurance Company:_____

Address:_____

Telephone:_____

Insurance Agent:_____

Telephone:_____

Location of Policy:_____

Linda M. Sekely, Esq.

(Please enclose a copy of the Insurance policy if available)

HEALTH INSURANCE

Effective Date:_____

Policy #:_____ I.D.#_____

Insurance Company:_____

Address:_____

Telephone:_____

Policy Contact:_____

Telephone:_____

Location of Policy:_____
(Please enclose a copy of the Insurance Document if available)

MEDICARE/MEDICAID

Application made for Medicare/Medicaid _____(Y/N)

Effective Date:_____ Card #:_____

Location of Card:_____
(Please attach copy of card)

_____

OTHER INSURANCE

_____

_____

_____

_____

HEALTH NSURANCE

Social Security Numbers:

Yours_____   Spouse_____

Location of Cards:_____
(Please attach copy of cards)

Social Security Benefits applied for at age:

You_____   Spouse_____

Date Benefits Started:

You_____   Spouse_____

Monthly Benefits as of 12/31/:

Yours_____   Spouse_____

Death benefits:_____

_____

Dependent Benefits:_____

_____

Note: Upon death, the surviving spouse, dependent children under the age of sixteen, or disabled children are usually entitled to Social Security benefits. To inquire about your Social Security benefits, call

Linda M. Sekely, Esq.

to file a claim as soon as possible to avoid the possibility of losing any benefit checks. Either the executor or spouse may call:

1 800 772 1213

LONG TERM CARE/NURSING HOME INSURANCE

Effective Date: _____

Policy #:_____ I.D.#_____

Insurance Company:_____

Address:_____

Telephone: _____

Contact Agent:_____

Telephone:_____

Location of Policy:_____
(Please enclose a copy of the Insurance Document if available)

VETERANS

Military Service:_____

Date of Discharge:_____

Location of Discharge Papers:_____

Insurance Coverage:_____

Health Benefits:_____

Burial Rights:_____

Note: To determine benefits upon Death, call the Veteran's Administration Nationwide number:

1 800 827-1000

Please have a copy of the Discharge papers, Marriage Certificate, Children's Birth Records, and the Death Certificate. Most cases can be handled by Telephone. The VA will send an application to determine survivor's eligibility and benefits.

HOMEOWNERS INSURANCE

Effective Date: _____

Policy Number:_____ I.D.#_____

Insurance Company:_____

Address: _____

Telephone:_____

Policy Contact:_____

Telephone:_____

Location of Policy:_____

AUTO INFO – INSURANCE

Effective Date:_____

Policy Number:_____ I.D.#_____

Insurance Company:_____

Address:_____

Telephone:_____

Policy Contact:_____

Telephone:_____

Location of Policy:_____

RESIDENCE

Type of Residence: House_____,   Townhouse_____,

Condominium_____,   Co-op_____,   Other____

Address:_____

Purchase Price:_____

Deed Located:_____

Name on Deed:_____

Mortgage held by:_____ Expected Payoff Date:_____

Location of Payment book:_____

Life Insurance on Mortgage?_____(Y/N) Policy#_____

Location of Policy_____

Agent:_____   Telephone:_____

Major improvements to property:

Date	Improvement	Approx. Cost
_____	_____	_____
_____	_____	_____
_____	_____	_____
_____	_____	_____
_____	_____	_____

_____   _____   _____

Do you have receipts to substantiate above costs?_____(Y/N)

Location:_____
(Attach copy of Settlement Sheet if Available)

SECONDARY RESIDENCE

Type of Residence: House_____,   Townhouse_____,

Condominium_____,   Co-op_____,   Other_____

Address:_____

Purchase Price:_____

Deed Located:_____

Name on Deed:_____

Mortgage held by:_____ Expected Payoff Date:_____

Location of Payment book:_____

Life Insurance on Mortgage?_____(Y/N) Policy#_____

Location of Policy_____

Agent:_____   Telephone:_____

Major improvements to property:

Date   Improvement   Approx. Cost

_____   _____   _____

_____   _____   _____

_____   _____   _____

_____   _____   _____

_____   _____   _____

_____   _____   _____

Do you have receipts to substantiate above costs?_____(Y/N)

Location:_____

(Attach copy of Settlement Sheet if Available)

Linda M. Sekely, Esq.

RENTAL PROPERTY

Description:_____

_____

Address:_____

Purchase Price:_____   Deed located:_____

Name of Joint/Co-owner(if any):_____

Management Company:_____

Contact Broker:_____   Telephone:_____

Tenant(s):_____

_____

Mortgage held by:_____

Are taxes included in Mortgage? ___(Y/N) Monthly Payment $___

Location of Payment book:_____

Life Insurance on Mortgage?_____(Y/N) Policy #:_____

Location of Policy:_____

Agent:_____ Telephone:_____

Major improvements to property:

Date   Improvement   Approx. Cost

_____   _____   _____

_____   _____   _____

Do you have receipts to substantiate above costs?_____(Y/N)

Location:_____

(Attach copy of Settlement Sheet if Available)

LAND

Description:_____

Address:_____

Purchase Price:_____ Deed located:_____

Name of Joint/Co-owner(if any):_____

Management Company:_____

Contact Broker:_____ Telephone:_____

Tenant(s):_____

_____

Mortgage held by:_____

Are taxes included in Mortgage? ___(Y/N) Monthly Payment $___

Location of Payment book:_____

Life Insurance on Mortgage?_____(Y/N) Policy #:_____

Location of Policy:_____

Agent:_____ Telephone:_____

Major improvements to property:

Date   Improvement   Approx. Cost

_____   _____   _____

_____   _____   _____

Do you have receipts to substantiate above costs?_____(Y/N)

Location:_____

(Attach copy of Settlement Sheet if Available)

Linda M. Sekely, Esq.

RETIREMENT PLANS

Type of Plan:

_____ Individual Retirement Account (IRA)
_____ Keogh
_____ 401(K) Plan
_____ Simplified Employee Pension (SEP)
_____ Employee Stock Ownership Plan (ESOP)
_____ Pension/Profit Sharing/Defined Benefit Plan
_____ Non-Qualified Retirement Plan
_____ Other

Name of Plan:_____

Institutions Assets Invested in:_____

Account Number:_____

Broker/Contact Agent:_____

Telephone:_____

Name of Participant:_____

Plan Beneficiaries:_____

Employer/Plan Sponsor:_____

Address:_____

Telephone:_____

Plan Trustee:_____ Telephone:_____

Have you received any Distributions?_____(Y/N) Date
Distributions began:_____

Annual Monthly Amount: $_____

Value of any loans taken against plan:$_____

Applicable interest rate on repayments:_____

RETIREMENT PLANS (PAGE 2)

Type of Plan:

_____	Individual Retirement Account (IRA)
_____	Keogh
_____	401(K) Plan
_____	Simplified Employee Pension (SEP)
_____	Employee Stock Ownership Plan (ESOP)
_____	Pension/Profit Sharing/Defined Benefit Plan
_____	Non-Qualified Retirement Plan
_____	Other

Name of Plan:_____

Institutions Assets Invested in:_____

Account Number:_____

Broker/Contact Agent:_____

Telephone:_____

Name of Participant:_____

Plan Beneficiaries:_____

Employer/Plan Sponsor:_____

Address:_____

Telephone:_____

Plan Trustee:_____ Telephone:_____

Have you received any Distributions?_____(Y/N) Date
Distributions began:_____

Annual Monthly Amount: $_____

Value of any loans taken against plan:$_____

Applicable interest rate on repayments:_____

Linda M. Sekely, Esq.

RETIREMENT PLANS (PAGE 3)

Type of Plan:

_____ Individual Retirement Account (IRA)
_____ Keogh
_____ 401(K) Plan
_____ Simplified Employee Pension (SEP)
_____ Employee Stock Ownership Plan (ESOP)
_____ Pension/Profit Sharing/Defined Benefit Plan
_____ Non-Qualified Retirement Plan
_____ Other

Name of Plan:_____

Institutions Assets Invested in:_____

Account Number:_____

Broker/Contact Agent:_____

Telephone:_____

Name of Participant:_____

Plan Beneficiaries:_____

Employer/Plan Sponsor:_____

Address:_____

Telephone:_____

Plan Trustee:_____ Telephone:_____

Have you received any Distributions?_____(Y/N) Date
Distributions began:_____

Annual Monthly Amount: $_____

Value of any loans taken against plan:$_____

Applicable interest rate on repayments:_____

Linda M. Sekely, Esq.

SAVINGS/BANK ACCOUNTS

_____ Checking _____ Savings _____Certificate of Deposit

Name(s) on the Account:_____

Bank:_____

Address:_____

Telephone:_____Account Number:_____

Statements are located:_____

_____ Checking _____ Savings _____Certificate of Deposit

Name(s) on the Account:_____

Bank:_____

Address:_____

Telephone:_____Account Number:_____

Statements are located:_____

_____ Checking _____ Savings _____Certificate of Deposit

Name(s) on the Account:_____

Bank:_____

Address:_____

Telephone:_____Account Number:_____

Statements are located:_____

CREDIT CARDS

_____ Visa   _____ Master Card _____ American Express

_____ Discover _____ Dept. Store Cards   _____ Other

Credit card Company:_____

Address:_____Telephone:_____

Name(s) on Card:_____

Account Number:_____   Expiration Date:_____

Card Location:_____

Statements are located:_____

_____ Visa   _____ Master Card _____ American Express

_____ Discover _____ Dept. Store Cards   _____ Other

Credit card Company:_____

Address:_____Telephone:_____

Name(s) on Card:_____

Account Number:_____   Expiration Date:_____

Card Location:_____

Statements are located:_____

CREDIT CARDS

_____ Visa _____ Master Card _____ American Express

_____ Discover _____ Dept. Store Cards _____ Other

Credit card Company:_____

Address:_____Telephone:_____

Name(s) on Card:_____

Account Number:_____ Expiration Date:_____

Card Location:_____

Statements are located:_____

_____ Visa _____ Master Card _____ American Express

_____ Discover _____ Dept. Store Cards _____ Other

Credit card Company:_____

Address:_____Telephone:_____

Name(s) on Card:_____

Account Number:_____ Expiration Date:_____

Card Location:_____

Statements are located:_____

MONEY OWED TO YOU

Issuer:_____
            (borrower)

Issued to:_____
           (owner of the note)

Face Amount of Note:$_____

Purchase Date:_____Purchase Price:_____

Location of Note:_____

Expected Payoff Date:_____

(Attach Copies if Available)

Issuer:_____
            (borrower)

Issued to:_____
           (owner of the note)

Face Amount of Note:$_____

Purchase Date:_____Purchase Price:_____

Location of Note:_____

Expected Payoff Date:_____

(Attach Copies if Available)

STOCKS/BONDS/INVESTMENTS

Brokerage Company:_____

Broker Contact: _____

Address:_____

Telephone:_____

Name(s) on Account:_____

Recent year-end Statements Attached:_____(Y/N)   Location   of
Statements_____

Brokerage Company:_____

Broker Contact: _____

Address:_____

Telephone:_____

Name(s) on Account:_____

Recent year-end Statements Attached:_____(Y/N)   Location   of
Statements_____

Brokerage Company:_____

Broker Contact: _____

Linda M. Sekely, Esq.

Address:_____

Telephone:_____

Name(s) on Account:_____

Recent year-end Statements Attached:_____(Y/N) Location of
Statements_____

MUTUAL FUNDS
(Not Held with Brokerage Account)

Company:_____

Agent:_____

Telephone:_____

Name on the Account:_____

Is Income reinvested?_____(Y/N)

If income is *not* being reinvested, where are the dividends sent?

_____

Recent year-end Statements Attached:_____(Y/N)

Location of Statements:_____

Company:_____

Agent:_____

Telephone:_____

Name on the Account:_____

Is Income reinvested?_____(Y/N)

If income is *not* being reinvested, where are the dividends sent?

_____

Linda M. Sekely, Esq.

Recent year-end Statements Attached:_____(Y/N)

Location of Statements:_____

STOCKS/BONDS/INVESTMENTS
(Not Held with Brokerage Account)

Stocks/Certificates/Bonds

Company: _____

Names on Certificate(s):_____

Number of Shares_____

Certificate Number(s):_____

Purchase Date:_____   Purchase Price:_____

Location of Certificates:_____
(attach copies if available)

Stocks/Certificates/Bonds

Company: _____

Names on Certificate(s):_____

Number of Shares_____

Certificate Number(s):_____

Purchase Date:_____   Purchase Price:_____

Location of Certificates:_____
(attach copies if available)

BUSINESS INTERESTS

Name of the Business Entity:

_____

Description of Entity:_____

Type of Entity:

_____Partnership   _____Limited Liability Corporation
_____Corporation   _____Limited Liability Partnership
_____S Corporation   _____Professional Corporation
_____Sole Proprietor   _____Other (Specify)_____

Address of the Entity:_____

Telephone:_____

Contact Person to call:_____

Location of Shareholder or Buy/Sell Agreement:_____

═══

Name of the Business Entity:

_____

Description of Entity:_____

Type of Entity:

_____Partnership   _____Limited Liability Corporation
_____Corporation   _____Limited Liability Partnership
_____S Corporation   _____Professional Corporation
_____Sole Proprietor   _____Other (Specify)_____

Address of the Entity:_____

Telephone:_____

Contact Person to call:_____

Location of Shareholder or Buy/Sell Agreement:_____

INDIVIDUAL TAXES

INDIVIDUAL TAX RETURNS

Name of Preparer:_____

Company:_____   Telephone:_____

Location of Federal and State Tax Returns:_____

GIFT TAX RETURNS

Have you filed Gift Tax returns in the past? _____(Y/N)
(Form 709)

Years Gift Tax Returns filed?   ___   ___   ___   ___

Location of prior year tax returns _____

I have made the following gifts in the current year 20___.

Name:_____   Name:_____

Relationship:_____   Relationship:_____

Social Security #:_____   Social Security #:_____

Nature of Gift:_____   Nature of Gift:_____

Amount $_____   Amount $_____

I have made the following gifts in the current year 20___.

Name:_____   Name:_____

Relationship:_____   Relationship:_____

Social Security #:_____   Social Security #:_____

Nature of Gift:_____   Nature of Gift:_____

Amount $_____   Amount $_____

QUICK ESTATE CHECKLIST

The following checklist should be used as a guideline to assist you in carrying out the wishes of your deceased. It was prepared in order to save you hours of work and emotional anguish. It is not exclusive and should be updated on a regular basis.

_____Call relative, friend, executor to help.

_____Call family, friends, religious leader

_____Call employer

_____Call Financial Advisors, Inc.

_____Call lawyer, advisors, etc.

_____Call business associates

_____Call funeral director

_____Call hospital/doctor regarding autopsy, anatomical gifts, etc.

_____Obtain 10-12 copies of death certificate

_____Notify bank about bank accounts, certificates of deposit, etc.

_____Notify mortgage companies/landlord (if renting)

_____Collect and file last illness expenses and funeral expenses

_____Advise Social Security Office (or Veteran Administration if applicable)

_____Contact life insurance companies

_____Contact Investment bankers, security brokers, mutual fund brokers, etc.

_____Meet with Financial Advisors, Inc. and lawyers re: wills, trusts, tax filings, business agreements, estate valuation at date of death, distribution of assets, etc.

_____Consider changing or canceling the following services:

_____credit cards

_____utilities

_____post office box

_____magazines/newspapers

_____pets

_____other personal items

About the Author

Linda M. Sekely, Esq. is an experienced estate attorney who practices in her native Pennsylvania. A graduate of Duquesne University (Bachelor of Science in Business Administration) and the University of Pittsburgh School of Law, she is a national speaker and frequent guest lecturer for financial companies, regional conferences and professional associations. Linda is a published author of numerous articles on estate law. She is a faculty member of the Duquesne University Nonprofit Leadership Institute and is the founder and Executive Director of PEAT—Pennsylvania Estate Advocacy Team, a nonprofit estate educational service for the elderly community. Her advice column "Your Estate of Mind" appears regularly in regional professional newsletters. Linda hosts her own live weekly radio talk show, *Your Financial Connection*, where she advises listeners on matters of tax and estate planning.

Printed in the United States
17565LVS00005B/400-402